Contents

CALMING 2AM THOUGHTS

Your Survival Kit For Late-Night Overthinking

SATYA SANKAR SAHOO

Introduction

Ever found yourself lying awake at 2 AM, regretting a text you sent three years ago?

Or maybe your mind suddenly decides that *now* is the perfect time to analyze every awkward thing you've ever said?

Yeah, me too.

Welcome to the **2 AM Thought Spiral**, where logic goes to sleep, but your brain throws a full-blown anxiety party.

The world is quiet, distractions are gone, and suddenly, you're stuck inside your head—replaying past mistakes, worrying about the future, and questioning everything.

But here's the good news: **You're not alone.** And even better? There are ways to break free from this cycle.

This book isn't just about advice—it's about talking like old friends over a late-night cup of tea. I'll share real stories, practical tools, and some surprising wisdom from people who have been exactly where you are.

So, let's navigate these midnight thoughts together. 🖤

With understanding,
Satya Sankar Sahoo

Chapter 1

Understanding Your Midnight Anxiety

"You ever had a night where your thoughts wouldn't shut up?"

Kolkata at night has a different kind of magic. The streets, usually alive with honking yellow taxis, chai stalls buzzing with conversation, and trams lazily making their way through the city, are now eerily quiet. The air is thick with a faint scent of rain-soaked earth and the lingering aroma of biryani from some late-night kitchens in Park Street.

But none of that mattered to me.

I was lying in bed, staring at the ceiling fan that whirred softly above me. The dim blue glow from my phone screen was the only light in my room, and the time read **2:13 AM**.

I sighed. Another night lost to overthinking.

The thoughts wouldn't stop.

- *Why did I say that during the meeting today?*

- *What if I never figure out what I want in life?*

- *I should've replied differently to that message. Do they think I'm weird now?*

Tossing and turning, I wrapped the thin cotton sheet around me, only to throw it off again. I knew I needed sleep, but my brain was **running a marathon in the dark.**

That's when my phone buzzed.

A message from Aarav.

"Awake?"

I stared at it for a second. Aarav was my best friend since high school—the kind of guy who never seemed to worry about anything. While I was overanalyzing my life at 2 AM, he was probably up watching football highlights or scrolling through old music videos of Kishore Kumar.

I hesitated, then typed back.

"Yeah. Can't sleep."

A few seconds later, he replied:

"Let's go for a drive."

I sat up. A drive at 2 AM? Normally, I'd say no. But tonight, **anything felt better than being alone with my thoughts.**

A Midnight Escape Through Kolkata's Soul

Fifteen minutes later, I was in the passenger seat of Aarav's old silver Hyundai Santro, watching the quiet city roll past us. The streets, which would usually be packed with yellow Ambassador taxis and rickshaws during the day, were now empty except for the occasional chaiwala still serving his last few customers.

He turned down the music—some old RD Burman classic playing softly—and glanced at me.

"Alright, what's keeping you up this time?" Aarav asked as he steered onto the deserted Howrah Bridge, the Hooghly River shimmering underneath.

I sighed. "Everything."

He smirked. "That's specific."

I exhaled, watching the reflections of streetlights ripple on the water. "I don't know, man. My brain just doesn't stop. Every night, I lie in bed and suddenly start thinking about **everything**—the future, past mistakes, whether I'm doing enough, whether I'm good enough. It's exhausting."

Aarav was quiet for a moment, then asked, "Did I ever tell you about the time I almost didn't show up for my engineering entrance exam?"

I turned to him. "Wait, what? You're literally one of the smartest guys I know."

"Yeah," he said. "But that's not what my brain told me back then."

The Day Aarav Froze

Aarav took a deep breath before continuing.

"It was the night before my entrance exam. You know how hard I worked for that, right? But instead of sleeping, I was lying in bed **freaking out**. My brain was telling me I wasn't ready, that I was going to mess up, that maybe I wasn't as smart as everyone thought.

I kept thinking: *What if I fail? What if I ruin my future?*

And you know what I did?"

"What?"

"I walked out of my house at 2 AM, sat on the pavement near College Street, and just stared at the old bookshops lining the road. I seriously thought about not showing up for the exam at all."

"You were going to throw away years of hard work because of overthinking?" I asked, shocked.

"Yeah. That's what anxiety does to you." Aarav laughed bitterly. "It makes you doubt yourself even when you're fully capable. And back then, I had no idea how to deal with it. I felt trapped in my own mind."

The Warrior Who Wanted to Run Away

As we drove past Esplanade, with its grand colonial buildings now bathed in moonlight, Aarav turned to me.

"You ever heard the story of Arjuna from the Mahabharata?"

I blinked. "Uh… yeah, a little. He was the greatest warrior, right?"

"Exactly," Aarav nodded. "But do you know what happened to him right before the biggest battle of his life?"

I shrugged. "What?"

"He **froze.**"

I turned to him. "Wait. What?"

Aarav grinned. "Yeah. **The most powerful warrior of his time completely broke down.** He stood in the middle of the battlefield, saw his enemies lined up, and suddenly started **overthinking everything.** He started doubting whether he could fight, questioning if he was even doing the right thing, worrying about every possible consequence."

I raised an eyebrow. "Sounds familiar."

Aarav smirked. "Exactly. **You're fighting a war against your own thoughts.** And right now, your brain is acting like Arjuna before Krishna knocked some sense into him."

I let that sink in.

The 90-Second Rule & Letting Go of the Spiral

Aarav pulled the car over near Princep Ghat. The old pillars stood tall against the river, a few college students sitting quietly on the steps, lost in their own worlds.

"You know what I did when I was freaking out before my exam?" Aarav said, watching the ripples in the river.

"What?"

"I gave myself 90 seconds."

I frowned. "What do you mean?"

"There's something called the **90-Second Rule.** Neuroscientist **Dr. Jill Bolte Taylor** found that emotions—anxiety, regret, fear—only last **90 seconds** unless you keep fueling them with thoughts.

So I sat there and told myself: *Okay, I have 90 seconds to panic. I'm going to feel it fully. And after that, I'm letting it go."*

"And did it work?" I asked.

Aarav nodded. "It did. Because once you stop feeding your thoughts, they lose power."

I crossed my arms, thinking about my own 2 AM thoughts.

"Okay, but what if my brain **keeps** coming up with stuff?" I asked.

Aarav smirked. "Then you need to distract it. Give it something real to focus on. That's why meditation works. Or the **5-4-3-2-1 method.** Look around and name:

- **5** things you see
- **4** things you can touch
- **3** things you hear
- **2** things you smell
- **1** thing you taste

Your brain can't spiral when it's focused on the present."

💡 Midnight Takeaways (Quick Summary)

- Your brain overthinks at night because there are no distractions—it's not your fault.

- Even the strongest people (like Arjuna) doubt themselves before big moments.

- You have control over your actions, not the outcome. Stop obsessing over results.

- The 90-Second Rule: Emotions fade in 90 seconds unless you keep fueling them.

- When overthinking hits, focus on the present—ground yourself.

👣 What's Next?

Now that we understand **why** overthinking happens, how do we actually let go of those thoughts?

🚀 **Next Up → Chapter 2: The Art of Letting Go – A Midnight Conversation at Princep Ghat**

The Art of Letting Go – A Midnight Conversation at Princep Ghat

---

"Ever feel like your brain is holding you hostage?"

Princep Ghat at 3 AM had a strange kind of peace. The Hooghly River stretched ahead, reflecting the golden streetlights from the distant Howrah Bridge. The sound of gentle waves against the steps, the distant hum of a ferry cutting through the water—it all made the city feel like it was whispering its secrets.

Aarav and I were still sitting on the hood of his car, our unfinished coffee cups resting beside us. The night air was cool, but my mind was still warm with thoughts.

"So," Aarav said, stretching his arms behind his head, "do you believe me now? About how overthinking is basically a **mental battle** you keep fighting with yourself?"

I exhaled. "Yeah. But just knowing that doesn't make it easier to stop."

"Of course not," he said. "You can't just tell your brain to 'stop thinking.' That's like telling a cat to stop being curious."

I chuckled. "So what's the solution then, wise one?"

Aarav smirked. "Distraction, my friend. And maybe, the universe decides to help you in its own weird way."

And that's exactly when the universe sent **her.**

The Girl Who Interrupted Our Midnight Philosophy

"Seriously? You guys have been sitting here for the past 40 minutes and haven't even noticed me?"

We both turned at the voice, startled.

Standing behind us was **Riya.**

Now, let me introduce Riya. She wasn't just *any* girl. She was the **storm** in our trio. The kind of person who could argue for an hour about why Kolkata had the best street food in India and then get distracted by a street puppy and forget the argument entirely.

She was fearless, unpredictable, and somehow always managed to appear when we least expected her.

"What the hell are you doing here at this hour?" I asked, still surprised.

She crossed her arms, tilting her head. "I could ask you the same thing. But let me guess—you two were sitting here, talking about life, the meaning of existence, and how overthinking ruins everything?"

Aarav laughed. "She knows us too well."

I shook my head, grinning. "What about you?"

Riya plopped herself onto the hood of the car next to us, stealing Aarav's half-finished coffee. "Well, I was driving back from my cousin's wedding in Salt Lake when I saw Aarav's car here. I thought, *either they're planning a heist, or they're having one of their deep existential conversations.* Figured I'd crash the party."

"And here we thought we were having a peaceful, introspective night," Aarav teased.

"Introspection is overrated," she said, taking a sip of coffee. "Besides, overthinking is just a fancy way of telling yourself stories that aren't even true."

I raised an eyebrow. "What do you mean?"

The Elephant and the Rope

Riya stretched her legs, letting her boots rest against the front bumper of the car. "You know, when I was a kid, my dad once took me to see this small circus in the outskirts of Kolkata. I was fascinated by the elephants there, but something weird caught my attention."

She turned to us, her eyes gleaming in the dim light. "The elephants were huge, right? Easily strong enough to break free. But they were tied with these tiny ropes around their ankles. I kept wondering—why don't they just break free?"

I frowned. "Why didn't they?"

Riya smirked. "Because when they were babies, those same ropes **were strong enough** to hold them back. They tried to escape, but they weren't strong enough yet. And after failing so many times, they just *stopped trying*. Even when they grew big and strong, they still believed they were trapped. Their minds convinced them that escape was impossible."

I stared at her. "Holy shit."

"Exactly." She leaned back, letting the night air brush against her face. "That's what overthinking does to us. We keep telling ourselves the same **limiting stories**—'I'm not good enough,' 'I'll never figure things out,' 'I'm stuck'—and we **believe them**, even when they're not true anymore."

The Art of Letting Go

Aarav whistled. "Damn, Riya. I think you just hijacked this conversation and took it to a whole new level."

She shrugged. "Look, all I'm saying is, our thoughts are just thoughts. They don't define us. The only way to stop overthinking is to **realize when we're trapped in our own mental circus.**"

I exhaled, staring at the river. "So how do we break free from the rope?"

"By questioning it," she said simply. "By asking ourselves: *Is this thought actually true? Is this thought helping me? Would I still believe this if I wasn't scared?*"

Aarav nodded. "So basically, instead of fighting overthinking, we should **observe it and challenge it.**"

"Exactly." Riya smiled. "You can't stop thoughts from coming. But you can decide whether to believe them."

I thought about my own thoughts—the *'I'm not doing enough'* ones, the *'What if I fail?'* ones. **Were they even real? Or just a rope I was never strong enough to break before?**

Maybe, just maybe, I was strong enough now.

📝 Midnight Exercises: Try This Tonight

☑ The Thought Audit

- Grab a notebook. Write down the **three thoughts** that bother you most at night.

- Ask yourself: **Is this thought true, or is it just an old fear?**

- Rewrite the thought in a way that **empowers you instead of limiting you.**

☑ The 10-Minute Release

- Set a timer for **10 minutes.**

- Write down **everything on your mind**—no filters.

- When the timer stops, **close the notebook and let it go.**

☑ The Rope Test

- Next time you catch yourself overthinking, ask:

  - **Is this thought actually true, or is it a past belief?**

  - **What would I do if I wasn't afraid?**

  - **If this wasn't my thought, but my best friend's—what would I tell them?**

⚲ Midnight Takeaways (Quick Summary)

- **Overthinking is just storytelling. But not all stories are true.**

- **Like elephants tied with weak ropes, we believe in limits that don't exist anymore.**

- **The key to letting go is to question our thoughts, not fight them.**

- **You can't stop thoughts from coming, but you can decide whether to believe them.**

👣 What's Next?

Tonight, I learned something important: **letting go isn't about forcing thoughts away. It's about realizing they were never real to begin with.**

But the night wasn't over yet.

As we sat there, watching the sun slowly rise over Kolkata, Riya suddenly turned to me and said,

"Okay, since we're all up, who's up for some early morning chai at Sharma's Tea Stall?"

I laughed. **The night started with overthinking, but it was ending with chai, friends, and the realization that maybe—just maybe—my thoughts weren't as powerful as I once believed.**

🚀 **Next Up → The Overthinker's Toolkit – Chai, Chaos & A Crash Course in Letting Go**

Chapter 3

The Overthinker's Toolkit – Chai, Chaos & A Crash Course in Letting Go

---

"Sometimes, all you need to stop overthinking is a good cup of chai."

By the time we reached **Sharma's Tea Stall** near Ballygunge, the city was slowly waking up. The early-morning crowd had started gathering—milkmen delivering fresh bottles, newspaper vendors cycling past, and cab drivers taking their first sips of chai before a long day.

The air was thick with the scent of cardamom tea and the distant aroma of kathi rolls being prepared at a nearby stall.

We grabbed three small earthen **kulhads** of tea and found a quiet corner to sit. The warmth of the chai seeped into my fingers, and for the first time that night, my mind felt... still.

Riya took a sip and sighed. "You know, chai at dawn just hits different."

Aarav grinned. "Agreed. Now, back to business—before we got distracted by the story of circus elephants, we were talking about **how to actually stop overthinking.**"

I rolled my eyes. "Right, because I totally want to have a life lesson at 5 AM."

Riya smirked. "Oh, don't worry, we'll keep it **entertaining.** Welcome to—" she paused dramatically, "The Overthinker's Toolkit: Kolkata Edition."

The "What's the Worst That Could Happen?" Game

Riya leaned forward. "Alright, let's start with a game. You overthink because your brain keeps throwing worst-case scenarios at you, right?"

I nodded. "Yeah. Like, *What if I mess up that presentation tomorrow?* or *What if I say something dumb?*"

"Cool. Now let's play **The Worst That Could Happen.** Say your worry out loud, and let's actually take it to its extreme."

I hesitated. "Fine. Let's say I mess up my presentation tomorrow."

Aarav grinned. "Alright. So, worst case?"

"I forget my points and blank out."

Riya smirked. "And then?"

"My boss thinks I'm unprepared."

"And then?"

"Uh… maybe I don't get that promotion?"

"And then?"

"I guess I'll still have my job… just not a great impression?"

Riya leaned back, satisfied. "Exactly. You started with 'I'm doomed,' but the **actual worst-case scenario** is… a mildly awkward moment that you'll forget in a week."

I blinked. "Oh."

Aarav laughed. "See? Overthinking **magnifies problems.** This game helps shrink them back to reality."

The "Flip the Script" Trick

Aarav tapped his kulhad against mine. "Now, let's try this—**flip your thought into something empowering.**"

I frowned. "Like what?"

"Like, instead of thinking *What if I fail?*, you ask, *What if I succeed?*"

Riya chimed in, "Instead of *I'm not good enough*, try *I am still learning, and that's okay.*"

I stared at them. "You two have really turned my breakdown into a TED Talk, huh?"

They both laughed.

The "Will This Matter in 5 Years?" Rule

Riya pointed at the chai stall owner. "You think Sharmaji remembers what he was worried about five years ago?"

I shook my head. "Probably not."

"Exactly." She smirked. "And neither will you."

Aarav grinned. "So whenever you overthink something, ask: **Will this matter in 5 years?** If the answer is no, don't waste **5 minutes** stressing over it."

The "Brain Dump" Method

I sipped my chai, letting the warmth settle in my chest. "Alright, but what if my brain just **won't shut up**?"

Aarav set his cup down. "Ever tried the **brain dump method**?"

"Sounds messy."

"It's simple. **Before bed, write down every single thought in your head.** Don't filter it, don't make it neat. Just dump it all onto a page."

"And then?"

"And then shut the notebook and tell yourself, *I'll deal with this tomorrow.* It tricks your brain into **letting go.**"

I thought about it. "I like that. My mind feels like a cluttered room. Maybe writing it down is like organizing the mess."

The 5-4-3-2-1 Grounding Trick

Riya stretched her arms. "And finally, my favorite—**the 5-4-3-2-1 trick.**"

I raised an eyebrow. "Sounds like a countdown to a rocket launch."

She grinned. "It kinda is. It **launches you out of overthinking** and into reality."

She explained:

- **5 things you can see** (*the chai stall, the streetlight, Aarav's horrible hairstyle...*)

- **4 things you can touch** (*the cup, the bench, the scarf around my neck...*)

- **3 things you can hear** (*the distant honking, someone sweeping the sidewalk, Riya's voice...*)

- **2 things you can smell** (*the chai, the faint scent of wet earth...*)

- **1 thing you can taste** (*the last sip of chai...*)

"By the time you're done, your mind has **shifted out of overthinking mode** and back into the present moment," she finished.

The Sun Rises Over Kolkata

As we finished our tea, the first light of dawn painted the city in soft orange hues. The Howrah Bridge glowed in the distance, and I could hear the faint call of vendors setting up their stalls for the morning rush.

For the first time in a long time, I felt... light.

"So," Aarav said, stretching. "Think you can handle your overthinking better now?"

I nodded. "I think I have a few weapons in my toolkit now."

Riya grinned. "Good. Now, what's next?"

I thought for a second, then smirked. "How about breakfast at Flurys?"

Aarav gasped. "Bro, do you know how expensive Flurys is? We're still broke!"

Riya rolled her eyes. "Relax. **I got this one.** Let's go before the city wakes up."

And just like that, **we piled into the car, heading toward another unexpected morning adventure.**

As we drove, I glanced at the rising sun over the Howrah Bridge, feeling something, I hadn't felt in a long time—**light.**

The thoughts would still come. The overthinking wouldn't magically disappear.

But now? **I knew how to handle them.**

👣 What's Next?

I learned that night that **overthinking isn't the enemy—it's just a bad habit.** And like any habit, **it can be broken.**

But we weren't done yet. Because as I would soon realize, there was one more battle left—**the social media trap.**

🚀 **Next Up → A Day in the Life – The Office, A Bus Ride & The Social Media Trap**

Chapter 4

A Day in the Life – The Office, A Bus Ride & The Social Media Trap

---

"Some days start normal. Until they don't."

It was just another ordinary day in Kolkata. The kind where nothing seems special at first. The city was waking up to its usual rhythm—yellow taxis swerving through streets, vendors setting up their stalls, and the smell of freshly made singhara filling the morning air.

I had barely managed to drag myself out of bed, already dreading the long day ahead. Work had been piling up, and I knew my boss, Mr. Chatterjee, would have his usual **Monday-morning scowl** on full display.

Still half-asleep, I made my way to the bus stop, a steaming cup of roadside **cha** in my hand. My phone vibrated in my pocket. I pulled it out, already expecting a work email.

Instead, it was a message from **Aisha.**

Aisha: "Where are you? The office feels like a funeral without you."

I smirked and typed back.

Me: "Stuck in Monday traffic. Tell Chatterjee I died on my way to work."

Aisha: "Noted. Will ask for a day off in your honor."

Aisha had been my colleague for two years now, and somehow, we had survived this job together. She was the only thing that made **boring office hours bearable.**

As I took another sip of tea, a familiar voice snapped me out of my morning daze.

"You look like a man who just realized it's **not Friday.**"

I turned to see **Tanya** grinning at me.

Tanya was a junior designer in our company, someone I had worked with but never really gotten to know well. She had a way of always looking effortlessly put together—while I was out here trying (and failing) to not look like I had barely slept.

"You caught me," I admitted. "I woke up hoping for a Saturday, but life had other plans."

She laughed as the bus rolled in. "C'mon. Let's suffer together."

The Bus Ride & The Problem With Mondays

We found a spot near the window as the bus rattled through the city. Outside, the streets of Kolkata were a blend of chaos and charm—college students rushing to class, office-goers squeezing past each other, hawkers balancing stacks of newspapers on their heads.

"So, what's today's disaster?" Tanya asked, pulling out her phone.

"Meeting at 10 AM," I muttered. "Chatterjee's going to grill me for no reason."

She winced. "Sounds painful."

I sighed. "Yeah, well, that's work."

Tanya, meanwhile, was scrolling through Instagram, and within minutes, I saw her face **completely change.**

She had that familiar expression—the one we all get when social media suddenly makes us feel like **our lives are... less.**

"What happened?" I asked.

She hesitated, then turned her screen toward me.

It was a picture of someone we both vaguely knew—a college acquaintance who had just moved abroad for a job. The caption read:

"New city, new job, new beginnings! 🍁 ✈ Feeling on top of the world!"

Tanya exhaled sharply. "You ever look at these posts and feel like... you're not doing enough?"

I thought about it. "Yeah. All the time."

She locked her phone and sighed. "I know social media is just a highlight reel, but sometimes it still gets to me."

The "Everyone Has Their Life Together Except Me" Illusion

"You know," I said, "there's this thing called **The Spotlight Effect.** Basically, we think people are watching and judging our lives way more than they actually are. We assume everyone has their life figured out—except us."

Tanya raised an eyebrow. "And?"

"And it's **bullshit.**"

I gestured toward the people in the bus. "Look around. Every single person here has their own worries, their own struggles. But you don't see it on social media. You only see the wins, the filtered versions."

Tanya was quiet for a moment. Then she nodded. "Yeah... I guess you're right."

She glanced at her phone one last time before shoving it into her bag. "I hate that one Instagram post just ruined my morning."

I shrugged. "You let it, that's all. Happens to all of us."

The Office, The Chaos & The Unexpected Lesson

When we reached the office, Aisha was already waiting at my desk, arms crossed.

"You made it," she said dramatically. "I was just about to file a missing person report."

I rolled my eyes. "I appreciate the concern."

Tanya walked off to her side of the office, and I was just about to start my day when I heard a voice from behind.

"Meeting room. Now."

I turned slowly.

There he was. **Mr. Chatterjee.**

If Tanya had FOMO from Instagram, I had **PTSD from my boss.**

The Meeting That Wasn't As Bad As I Thought

Inside the meeting room, Chatterjee went on one of his usual rants—something about deadlines, clients, and efficiency. I nodded along, fully expecting to be **chewed out.**

But then, something weird happened.

Instead of panicking, I thought about **Tanya's reaction to Instagram this morning.**

She had let a single post mess with her whole day—just like how I let these meetings ruin mine.

I realized, **Chatterjee's words weren't personal.** They were just noise. Work stress was just another illusion—like social media, but with fewer filters and worse lighting.

And just like that, the meeting didn't seem that terrifying anymore.

The Evening Walk & A New Perspective

At the end of the day, I ran into Tanya again as I was leaving.

"Still thinking about that Instagram post?" I asked.

She smiled. "Nope. You?"

"About what?"

She rolled her eyes. "The Chatterjee disaster."

I shrugged. "It was just another meeting. No big deal."

She smirked. "Wow. Look at us. Evolving."

We walked toward the bus stop together, the streets of Kolkata now bathed in golden evening light. The city was alive again—vendors selling puchkas, friends laughing outside tea stalls, rickshaws weaving through traffic.

And I thought to myself:

💭 *Maybe we all get too caught up in illusions—on screens, in offices, in our own heads. Maybe life is just happening, and we forget to notice it.*

For the first time in a long time, I put my phone away.

Just for a while.

Just to be here.

📌 Key Takeaways from Today's Chaos

- **Social media shows the highlights, not the whole picture.**

- **Everyone feels like they're behind, but no one actually is.**

- **Work stress, like social media, is just noise—it doesn't define your worth.**

- **Sometimes, putting your phone away is the best thing you can do for your mind.**

👣 What's Next?

That evening, I sat by my window, watching the city lights flicker.

I thought about the day—the unnecessary Instagram stress, the pointless office panic, and how much of it was just **self-created.**

And I wondered...

If I could let go of this, **what else could I let go of?**

🚀 **Next Up → Chapter 5: Reframing Your Thoughts – Dealing with Regret, Fear, and What-Ifs**

Chapter 5

Reframing Your Thoughts – Dealing with Regret, Fear, and What-Ifs

Kolkata at night was a different city. The chaos of the day dissolved into something softer. The yellow taxis slowed down, the trams took their final rounds, and the air smelled of old books, wet earth, and the last batch of singaras frying in oil at the chai stalls.

I, however, was still **very much awake.**

It was well past **1 AM**, and I had been trying to sleep for an hour. But no matter how hard I tried—closing my eyes, shifting positions, adjusting my pillow for the tenth time— **my mind just wouldn't shut up.**

I had gone through the whole **Overthinker's Nightly Routine™:**

▦ **Step 1:** Scroll Instagram mindlessly.

♫ **Step 2:** Play soft music to relax.

💭 **Step 3:** Get attacked by memories of embarrassing moments from six years ago.

🔄 **Step 4:** Overanalyze everything I said today.

And now, I was stuck in **Step 5:** Wondering if I would ever get a normal night's sleep again.

Frustrated, I got out of bed and walked to my window, looking out at the city. Below, the streets stretched long and empty, lit only by the flickering streetlights and the occasional passing taxi. A stray dog curled up near a tea stall, a few night-shift workers stood sipping chai, and the distant sound of a train rumbling over the Howrah Bridge filled the air.

I sighed.

This wasn't just tonight. **This was every night.**

A Taxi Ride & An Unplanned Encounter

On impulse, I grabbed my hoodie, slipped into my sneakers, and stepped out.

I didn't have a destination—I just **needed to move.** Maybe a walk would tire me out. Maybe fresh air would clear my mind.

As I wandered aimlessly, I reached a small roadside tea stall near College Street, the kind that stayed open all night for students pulling all-nighters and rickshaw pullers taking a break. The old man running the stall looked up.

"Late night, beta?" he asked, pouring chai into a small earthen **kulhad**.

I sighed. "Yeah. Couldn't sleep."

He nodded knowingly. "The city doesn't sleep either. But she knows how to rest."

Before I could respond, an old yellow taxi pulled up beside me, its engine purring softly. The driver, an elderly man with a thick white beard, leaned out the window.

"You need a ride?"

I shook my head. "Just out for a walk."

He studied me for a moment, then smiled. "Or maybe you need a conversation."

I hesitated. Then, for some reason, I nodded. "Maybe."

"Come, sit," he said, tapping the passenger seat.

Normally, I wouldn't just get into a stranger's taxi at 2 AM, but something about him—his calmness, his familiarity—made me trust him.

So I got in.

Yusuf – The Man Who Learned to Sleep

We drove slowly through the quiet streets of Kolkata. The city, which during the day roared with life, now felt like it was exhaling.

"You don't sleep much, do you?" Yusuf, the driver, asked.

I sighed. "I try. My mind doesn't listen."

He chuckled. "Ah. The **midnight chatter.** I know it well."

I glanced at him. "Yeah?"

He nodded. "I was like you once. Spent years believing sleep was a waste of time. Thought I could survive on work, money, and a strong cup of chai."

I leaned back, interested. "What changed?"

He took a deep breath, eyes on the road. "A near-death experience."

That got my attention.

The Night Yusuf Almost Didn't Wake Up

Yusuf had spent **30 years driving taxis in Kolkata.**

For years, he worked almost **20 hours a day**, barely resting. At night, when he finally got home, his mind wouldn't shut down. He'd overthink—about money, about his family, about whether he had saved enough for his children's future.

One day, he had been driving for **17 hours straight**, exhausted but determined to make a little extra money.

A passenger got in near Park Circus and asked him to drop him at Jadavpur. It was a routine ride—until Yusuf **fell asleep at the wheel.**

"For a second," he said, "I **closed my eyes.** And when I opened them, I had swerved into the wrong lane."

He barely missed hitting a truck.

The passenger screamed. Yusuf apologized. But something inside him **shifted that night.**

He pulled over, told the passenger to take another cab, and went home. And for the first time in years, he **slept like his life depended on it.**

Because it did.

The Da Vinci Sleep Myth & Why We Get It Wrong

As we passed through Esplanade, Yusuf asked, "You know Leonardo da Vinci?"

I nodded. "Of course."

"People say he never slept properly. Just **20-minute naps every few hours.**"

I frowned. "And it worked?"

"For a while," Yusuf admitted. "But eventually, it caught up with him. His body, his mind—it all slowed down. You can't cheat sleep forever."

I let that sink in. "So even geniuses can't outsmart sleep?"

"No one can," Yusuf said. "The brain needs rest. If you don't give it, it will take it from you. The body always collects its debt."

I stared at the road ahead, thinking about my own sleepless nights. Was I really **choosing productivity over sleep, or was I just trapped in a cycle I didn't know how to break?**

How I Finally Slept That Night

As Yusuf dropped me back home, I asked, "What's your secret? How do you sleep now?"

He smiled. "I have three rules."

Rule 1: No screens before sleep.

"Your phone is like the sun—it keeps your brain awake."

Rule 2: Empty the mind.

"Write down your worries before bed. That way, your mind doesn't feel like it has to keep them all night."

Rule 3: Breathe like a sleeping man.

"Slow, deep breaths. Inhale for 4 seconds, hold for 7, exhale for 8."

That night, I followed his advice.

And for the first time in a long time...

I **slept.**

Try This Tonight – The Sleep Reset

The "Screen-Free Hour" Rule

- Put your phone away **1 hour before bed.**

- Read a book, take a shower, or just sit quietly.

☑ **The "Write & Release" Method**

- Write down your biggest worries **before bed.**

- Close the notebook and tell yourself, *This can wait till tomorrow.*

☑ **The 4-7-8 Breathing Trick**

- Inhale for **4 seconds.**

- Hold for **7 seconds.**

- Exhale for **8 seconds.**

- Repeat. Your body will relax.

⚗ Key Takeaways from Yusuf & Da Vinci

- **Sleep isn't a waste of time—it's how your brain recharges.**

- **You can't function on exhaustion forever. One day, your body will force you to stop.**

- **Overthinking at night is a habit. But it can be replaced with better habits.**

- **The quality of your sleep determines the quality of your life.**

👣 What's Next?

That night, as I drifted off, I thought about Yusuf and his near-accident.

And I realized—**we always think we have time to rest later. But later never comes unless we choose it.**

And for the first time in years, I chose rest.

🚀 **Next Up → The Festival, The Saree, and A Night to Remember**

Chapter 6

The Festival, The Saree, and A Night to Remember

"Some nights are meant to be remembered. Others? Well, they remind you why you should never trust your friends with your social calendar."

The Invitation That Left No Room for Excuses

It started with an email.

Not the usual *URGENT: Deadline Extended* or *Reminder: Client Presentation* kind of email. This one was different.

Subject: Durga Puja Office Get-Together – Attendance Encouraged.

I knew what that meant: *Skip at your own risk, but people will notice.*

Before I could decide whether I wanted to attend, a familiar voice broke my train of thought.

"You're coming, right?"

I looked up to see **Aisha,** arms folded, giving me the *I dare you to say no* look.

"Aisha's life motto: If you're not suffering for a festival, you're not doing it right."

Right behind her, leaning against my desk like he had all the time in the world, was **Ritwik.**

Now, Ritwik was the kind of guy who **somehow made every situation look effortless.** He could walk into a stressful board meeting with a cup of coffee in one hand, crack a joke in the first two minutes, and leave with **half the room charmed and the other half wondering how he got promoted twice in one year.**

"Durga Puja, dude," Ritwik said casually. "It's illegal to miss it in Kolkata. You don't want to get banned from the city, do you?"

I sighed. "Look, I—"

Aisha cut me off. "Don't even try. You're coming. No excuses."

Ritwik smirked. "I mean, let the man speak. Maybe he has some deep, philosophical reason for wanting to sit at home and stare at his ceiling instead."

I gave him a look. "You both are exhausting."

"Yes, and yet, here we are, still your friends," Aisha said.

I exhaled. "Fine. I'll come."

Ritwik patted my shoulder. "See? That wasn't so hard."

Aisha grinned. "Oh, it gets better. You actually have to **dress well** for this."

"Okay, now you're asking for too much."

The Saree, The Kurta, and Ritwik's Fashion Commentary

Durga Puja night arrived **faster than expected.**

I reached the pandal **on time, which was already an achievement.** The place was alive—**dhaak beats vibrated in the air, fairy lights flickered above the crowd, and the smell of incense mixed with the unmistakable scent of deep-fried street food.**

Then I spotted Aisha.

She was wearing a **deep maroon saree**, draped effortlessly, silver jhumkas swaying as she turned to talk to someone. She looked different—not in the overdone, dramatic movie way, but in a way that made me realize **I'd only ever seen her in rushed office meetings and sarcastic conversations.**

And then, of course, she caught me staring.

"Yes?" she asked, raising an eyebrow.

I cleared my throat. "Uh… you look… different."

She smirked. "That's the whole point. You, however…" She scanned my **simple white kurta** and shook her head. "Bare minimum effort."

"I'd like to think of it as *timeless simplicity*," I said.

Before she could reply, **Ritwik walked up, dramatically inspecting me like a fashion critic.**

"Ah, I see," he said, nodding seriously. "He's going for the *'I just escaped a client call but still showed up' aesthetic.* Very bold. Very corporate."

I rolled my eyes. "You two are ridiculous."

Aisha crossed her arms. "You say that like it's a surprise."

Navigating the Pujo Madness

The pandal was packed. People moved in **every possible direction,** the air thick with energy, excitement, and the occasional vendor shouting *"Ekdom garam singara!"*

As we made our way through the crowd, **Ritwik's survival instincts kicked in.**

"Alright, formation time," he said, stepping in front. "I'll clear the way."

"You're not parting the Red Sea," I muttered.

"You joke now, but let's see how you feel when you're stuck between an overly enthusiastic uncle and a selfie group."

To be fair, **he wasn't wrong.**

Somewhere between **dodging a group of women taking slow-motion saree videos and nearly getting smacked by a kid's flying balloon,** we finally made it to the front of the idol.

The air was **thick with the scent of camphor, marigold, and burning incense.** The dhaak beats felt almost alive, vibrating through my chest.

I turned to Aisha. **She had her eyes closed for a moment, hands folded, lost in a silent prayer.**

I had never seen her like this before.

Then she opened her eyes and caught me watching.

"What?" she asked.

"Nothing," I said quickly.

She smirked. "You totally just witnessed me being sentimental, didn't you?"

"I have no idea what you're talking about."

Before she could respond, Ritwik **reappeared with a plate of prasad.**

"Alright," he announced. "We survived the crowd, made our wishes, and—most importantly—**I found food.**"

"Life isn't always about big moments. Sometimes, it's just about being here."

I took the plate from him. "Your priorities are impressive."

He grinned. "I do my best."

The Realization I Didn't Expect

After prasad, we **headed to the food stalls,** because if there's one universal Pujo rule, it's **"Never leave without eating something fried."**

As we stood in line for kathi rolls, **Aisha turned to me.**

"You seem different tonight," she said.

I frowned. "What do you mean?"

"I don't know. **Less in your head.** More... here."

I thought about that.

She wasn't wrong. For once, I wasn't worrying about work. Or overthinking what I should say. Or wondering if I was **doing things right.**

I was just **existing.** And it felt—

"Wait. Are you... enjoying yourself?" Ritwik asked, narrowing his eyes in mock suspicion.

I sighed. "God forbid."

Aisha grinned. "I'm so proud. Our little overthinker is growing up."

Ritwik wiped an imaginary tear. "They grow up so fast."

"You two are the worst," I muttered.

They **burst out laughing.**

The Walk Back & The Thought That Stayed With Me

The crowd was **starting to thin,** the night slowly fading into **that peaceful, nostalgic phase of Pujo.**

As we walked out, **the sounds of dhaak beats softened behind us, mixing with the distant honking of yellow taxis.**

I turned to Aisha. "So, thanks for dragging me here."

She smirked. "Oh, it wasn't just me. Ritwik helped too."

Ritwik nodded. "Yep. I expect a formal letter of appreciation by tomorrow morning."

I laughed. "Not happening."

Aisha stretched her arms. "Well, we did it. Successfully survived an office outing."

I looked around. The festival, the people, the energy— everything felt **alive.**

I nodded. "Yeah. I think I'll actually remember this one."

And for once, **I didn't feel the need to overanalyze why.**

Key Takeaways from the Festival Night

- Sometimes, you need friends who force you out of your comfort zone.

- Not everything needs to be planned or analyzed. Some things are just meant to be lived.

- Overthinking pulls you out of life. Being present pulls you back in.

- Durga Puja is not just about traditions. It's about feeling alive, even if just for a night.

- You don't need a perfect reason to be happy. Some nights just give it to you.

Final Thought

As I headed home, **my mind wasn't racing.**

No spirals of doubt. Just the distant **echo of dhaak drums,** the soft flicker of fairy lights, and the quiet realization that **sometimes, life gives you moments too beautiful to overthink.**

And all you have to do is **let them happen.**

🚀 **Next Up → The Power of Perspective – Lessons from a Self-Made Man**

Chapter 7

The Power of Perspective – Lessons from a Self-Made Man

The café smelled of fresh coffee and rain-soaked pavement, a mix of nostalgia and warmth that belonged to old Kolkata. It was a quiet place, the kind where deals were made over filter coffee and unspoken thoughts hung between words.

I hadn't been here in years, but tonight, I had come for a reason.

Rahul Sen.

I had known him once, long before his name meant anything outside our small circle of friends. Now, he was something else. A name people whispered with admiration. A businessman who had built an empire from nothing. A man who had, somehow, figured it all out.

And yet, I couldn't shake the feeling that I wasn't supposed to be here.

I had almost turned back twice, but Rahul had texted before I could escape.

"If you're here, stop overthinking and walk in. I don't have all day."

Typical Rahul.

So I pushed open the glass door, stepping into the dimly lit café, the hum of conversation wrapping around me.

He was already there, sitting at the farthest table, sipping black coffee like it was the only thing keeping him alive. Same old Rahul. Crisp white shirt, sleeves rolled up, the kind of casual confidence that made people listen when he spoke.

"Finally," he said, not looking up. "I thought you got scared and ran."

I sat down, trying to ignore the way my brain was still screaming that I didn't belong in this conversation. "Almost did."

He smirked. "Figures."

I wasn't sure where to start. The reason I was here wasn't something I could put into words easily. It wasn't just about his success. It was about the fact that I was stuck. That overthinking had made every decision feel impossible, every risk too terrifying to take. And Rahul? He had never seemed like someone who hesitated.

"You look like you have a hundred thoughts in your head and no clue which one to trust," he said, watching me like he already knew everything I was thinking.

I exhaled. "How do you do it?"

He raised an eyebrow. "Do what?"

"Move forward," I said. "Make decisions without getting stuck in your own head. Not overthink everything."

Rahul leaned back, running a hand through his hair.

"You think I don't overthink?"

I frowned. "I don't know. Do you?"

He chuckled. "Let me tell you a story."

And just like that, the past unfolded between us.

"It was about five years ago," Rahul began, stirring his coffee absentmindedly.

"I had just started my business. A tiny office in an old building, barely enough money to pay my team. Every day was a struggle. We were chasing clients who never called back, writing proposals that went nowhere. And then, one night, everything almost fell apart."

I leaned in slightly, caught in the weight of his words.

"It was 2 AM," he continued. "I was in that tiny office, staring at a bank statement that looked like a joke. We were running out of money. I had invested everything into this company—my savings, my time, my sanity. And there I was, realizing I might have to shut it all down before it even got anywhere."

"Your mind can be a prison or a tool—it depends on whether you let thoughts trap you or push you forward."

He exhaled, shaking his head slightly as if remembering the sheer exhaustion of that night.

"I couldn't think straight. My brain was running in circles. What if I had made a mistake? What if I had wasted years of my life? What if I was about to fail, and everyone would know?"

I swallowed. I knew that feeling too well.

"But then," Rahul said, tapping his fingers against the table, "something happened."

I waited, but he didn't speak right away.

He just smiled slightly, like he could still see that moment in his mind.

"I stepped outside for some air," he said finally. "And right across the street, I saw this chaiwala. An old man, sitting by his tiny stall, making tea like he had done every night for years. He had a line of customers waiting. And I just stood there, watching him."

I frowned. "A chaiwala?"

Rahul nodded. "Yeah. This guy had none of my problems. No fancy office, no website, no investors. Just a kettle, some tea leaves, and a routine he had perfected over time. And yet, he was working. Selling one cup at a time, not worrying about ten years from now, not doubting if people would show up tomorrow. He was just doing what he knew."

He paused, letting the thought settle.

"That's when it hit me," he said, his voice quieter now. "Success isn't about knowing the future. It's about doing the next thing in front of you. One step at a time. No chaiwala sits there wondering, *What if people don't come tomorrow?* They just show up and work. And that's what I needed to do."

He took another sip of coffee, setting the cup down carefully.

"That was the night I stopped letting fear decide for me. I made the hardest decision of my life—I went home and slept."

"Clarity comes from action, not from endless thinking."

I blinked. "You… slept?"

He laughed. "Yeah. Because I realized **worrying wasn't going to put money in my account. Action would.** The next morning, I called every client we had ever pitched to. I found new ways to cut costs. I stopped hesitating. And slowly, things started working."

He leaned forward slightly, his voice firm now.

"The only real mistake? I almost let overthinking make me quit before I even tried properly."

I sat back, absorbing everything.

Rahul watched me for a moment before speaking again.

"You see, the problem isn't fear," he said. "Fear is normal. The problem is *not acting because of fear.*"

I nodded slowly. "So you're saying I should just… do things, even if I'm scared?"

Rahul smirked. "What else is there?"

I laughed under my breath. "It sounds too simple."

"That's the trick," he said. "It *is* simple. We just make it complicated."

He glanced at his watch. "Anyway, I have a meeting. But before I go, let me ask you one thing."

I looked up.

"What's the worst that can happen?" he asked.

I frowned. "What do you mean?"

"Whatever you're scared of," he said. "If you fail, if you make a mistake—what's the worst that can actually happen?"

I thought about it. "I guess… I'd have to start over."

Rahul nodded. "And?"

I hesitated. "And… I'd be embarrassed?"

He smiled. "And? Will you die? Will the world end?"

I sighed. "No."

"Exactly," he said, standing up. "So why are you letting it stop you?"

I had no answer.

Rahul clapped my shoulder. "You'll figure it out. Just stop waiting to feel ready."

And then he walked out, leaving me sitting there, staring at my coffee.

I had come looking for some big, complicated answer.

Instead, I had found something simple.

"Fear never goes away. But if you act anyway, it loses its power."

And maybe, that was all I needed to know.

Key Takeaways from Rahul's Story

- **Overthinking doesn't solve problems—action does.** Worrying about failure won't change the outcome. Doing something about it will.

- **Fear is normal. Letting fear stop you is the real mistake.** Every successful person feels fear. The difference? They move forward despite it.

- **You don't need to know the future. Just take the next step.** Like the chaiwala, focus on what's in front of you instead of stressing about what's ahead.

- **The worst-case scenario is rarely as bad as you think.** If you fail, you start over. Life moves on. The fear of failure is often worse than the failure itself.

- **You will never feel fully ready.** If you wait for confidence, you'll wait forever. Start before you feel prepared, and confidence will follow.

- **Sometimes, the best decision is to stop overthinking and just get some sleep.** Clarity comes when your mind is rested, not when you're stuck in a cycle of anxiety.

🚀 **Next Up → The Unexpected Joy That Changed Everything**

Chapter 8

The Unexpected Joy That Changed Everything

**"Sometimes, life doesn't give you what you want.
It gives you what you need—just when you
least expect it."**

Kolkata's morning **had it out for me.**

The **bus was packed beyond human limits,** the air **was thick with humidity,** and to make things worse, **I had just made a life-ruining discovery**—my inbox had betrayed me.

Client Presentation – 10 AM.

I checked the time. **9:37 AM.**

I checked my mental stability. **Non-existent.**

I could already imagine **Mr. Chatterjee's disappointment,** his sharp gaze scanning the room, realizing I hadn't even bothered to show up properly prepared.

By the time I reached the office, I was **sweaty, slightly breathless, and already ready to quit corporate life.** I tried to **sneak past reception,** hoping no one would notice.

I was wrong.

"Ah, finally decided to show up?"

I **froze.**

That voice could only belong to **one person.**

Mr. Chatterjee.

Standing **right near my desk, arms crossed, wearing his usual expression of deep judgment.**

"Sir, I—"

He sighed, **not in anger, but in something far worse—disappointment.** He reached into his hand and tossed a folder onto my desk.

"You have ten minutes to prepare," he said, adjusting his glasses.

I blinked. **Ten minutes?**

"For the presentation," he clarified, as if my brain was too slow to catch up.

My **stomach dropped.**

"Ten minutes?" I repeated, like maybe if I said it again, reality would shift.

"Yes," he said, tapping his watch. "Unless, of course, you'd like someone else to present your work."

His tone was **neutral**, but the challenge was **obvious.**

He didn't wait for my response. He just **walked off like a corporate villain,** leaving me staring at the folder like it had just **sentenced me to death.**

"Overthinking convinces you that failure is guaranteed. Reality, on the other hand, gives you a fighting chance."

Surviving the Meeting of Doom

The **conference room** felt **colder than usual** as I stepped inside.

Mr. Chatterjee was already seated at the head of the table, flanked by **two senior executives** and a **client who looked like he had no patience for nonsense.**

I felt my throat tighten. **The first words came out shaky.**

Then, something strange happened.

My **overthinking switched off.**

Maybe it was **sheer survival instinct**, but I just… **kept going.**

I knew this project inside out. I had worked on it for weeks. **Despite my panic, the words started flowing naturally.**

I kept my **voice steady, my tone confident, my thoughts clear.**

Halfway through, I **dared to glance at Mr. Chatterjee.** His face was unreadable.

Was he impressed? Was he silently drafting my termination letter? **I had no idea.**

When I **finally finished**, the room was **silent for a second.**

Then, to my absolute **shock,** the client **nodded approvingly.**

"That was well put," he said.

I **almost dropped my laptop.**

Mr. Chatterjee cleared his throat. "Yes. Good breakdown of the key points."

Wait.

Was that… **a compliment? From him?**

"Confidence isn't something you're born with. It's something you build—one success, one mistake at a time."

The Balcony Conversation That Changed Everything

The rest of the day felt **surreal.**

I wasn't anxious. **I wasn't replaying my every word. I** felt... **capable.**

And then, at **6:30 PM,** just as I was packing up, someone cleared their throat behind me.

I turned.

Mr. Chatterjee.

"Do you have a minute?" he asked.

I nodded, my **pulse suddenly erratic.**

He gestured toward the **office balcony.**

I had **never seen him there before.** So this? **This was new.**

The **evening air** was crisp as we stepped onto the **tiny office balcony**, the city stretching out below us.

"That was a good presentation today," he said.

I blinked. "Thanks, sir."

"You handled it well under pressure," he continued, leaning against the railing. "That's rare."

I hesitated. "I almost didn't."

He smirked. "I know. You overthink too much."

I exhaled. "It's a habit."

He nodded, **his eyes distant.** "I used to be the same."

I frowned. "You?"

"Yes," he said, watching the city lights flicker. "When I was younger, every decision felt like life or death. Every mistake haunted me. I spent nights obsessing over things that **never even mattered in the end.**"

I had **never seen this side of him.**

"What changed?" I asked.

He exhaled. "My first boss told me something I never forgot."

I waited.

"If you're making mistakes, it means you're doing something. The only people who never screw up are the ones too scared to try."

That hit **hard.**

"After that," he continued, "I stopped analyzing every mistake. I focused on *what's next* instead of *what went wrong*. And things changed."

I let his words **sink in.**

"So," he said, turning back to me, "are you going to keep overthinking, or are you going to start believing you're capable?"

I didn't have an answer.

Not yet.

But **something shifted inside me that evening.**

The city glowed beneath us, headlights and streetlamps blending into a soft haze. Kolkata had a different kind of beauty at night—**calmer, wiser, more forgiving.** Maybe that's what I needed to be too.

Mr. Chatterjee's words echoed in my head.

"Are you going to keep overthinking, or are you going to start believing you're capable?"

For the first time in my career, I didn't feel like I was just **passing through work, trying not to mess up.** I felt… important. Like maybe, just maybe, I wasn't just a replaceable employee.

I wanted to say something meaningful, something profound.

But before I could, Mr. Chatterjee checked his watch.

"Go home," he said. "And get some sleep for once."

That was the closest thing to *concern* I'd ever heard from him.

I didn't argue.

"Good night, sir," I said.

He nodded. "Good work today."

I walked away, not even **bothering to overthink what he meant.**

"Sometimes, one conversation is enough to change the way you see everything."

The Chaos That Is Aisha's House Party

By the time I got home, I was still **processing everything.**

And then my phone buzzed.

Aisha: *"House party. My place. Be here in 30 minutes. No excuses."*

I groaned. **Of course.**

Aisha had a talent for showing up in people's lives at the exact moment when they needed distraction. She was **chaotic, impulsive, borderline dangerous—but she knew how to make life feel less heavy.**

I almost typed out an excuse. **But then I stopped.**

A few hours ago, I had been **terrified of a meeting.** Now, I was just **grateful for today.**

I texted back.

"On my way."

Aisha's apartment **looked like a scene from a college movie.**

Music was blasting, people were laughing, and I was fairly certain someone was attempting to cook **with absolutely no idea how a stove worked.**

The first person I saw was **Tanya**, sitting on the couch, sipping what looked like a very questionable drink. She smirked the moment she spotted me.

"You survived another workday," she said.

"Apparently," I said, flopping onto the couch beside her.

"Wait, wait, wait," Aisha **appeared out of nowhere, eyes wide.** "You had the big presentation today, right? How did it go? Did Chatterjee destroy your soul?"

I hesitated.

"Actually… it went well," I said.

Aisha nearly **dropped her drink.**

"Wait, WHAT?!" she shrieked. "Hold on. **Did he smile? Did he give you a compliment?**"

"Well… not exactly a smile. More like **less of a scowl.** But yeah, he actually said I did good work."

Aisha grabbed Tanya's arm. "TELL ME YOU HEARD THAT. I'M NOT HALLUCINATING, RIGHT?!"

Tanya chuckled. "Trust me, we're all shocked."

Aarav, who had been busy inspecting the snacks, finally turned around. "Hold on. **Your boss gave you positive feedback?** This is historic. Are we celebrating?"

Aisha **threw her arms in the air.** "OF COURSE WE'RE CELEBRATING! THIS IS A NATIONAL HOLIDAY."

I laughed, shaking my head. **Only Aisha could turn my workday into a full-scale festival.**

The Difference Between Good Friends & Great Friends

The party continued, a **whirlwind of laughter, inside jokes, and near-disasters.**

At some point, Aisha **dragged me into a debate about whether Kolkata biryani was superior to Hyderabadi biryani.** I barely had time to react before **Aarav jumped in, passionately defending Hyderabadi cuisine like his life depended on it.**

Tanya, ever the peacekeeper, **rolled her eyes.** "You're all idiots. Eat what you like and shut up."

At one point, we ended up on the **balcony, drinks in hand, watching the city buzz below.**

"You seem different tonight," Tanya said, leaning against the railing.

I shrugged. "Do I?"

"Yeah," Aarav said. "Usually, after a long day, you're overthinking everything. But tonight, you're just… here."

I took a sip of my drink.

They weren't wrong.

Maybe it was **the meeting, maybe it was Mr. Chatterjee's words, or maybe it was this—being with people who made life feel lighter.**

"You know," I said, looking at the skyline, "I think I'm done worrying about things that don't matter."

Aisha gasped dramatically. "WHO ARE YOU AND WHAT HAVE YOU DONE WITH MY FRIEND?"

We all laughed, but deep down, I knew it was true.

For so long, I had been **caught in a cycle of stress, doubt, and overthinking.** But tonight?

Tonight, I felt **free.**

**"Cherish the small moments.
They're what make the big ones matter."**

The Walk Home & The Final Thought

The party lasted longer than I expected. **By the time I left, the city had settled into its midnight calm.**

Aisha was still **arguing with Aarav over food,** Tanya was making tea for herself, and the whole place looked like a **beautiful, chaotic mess.**

As I stepped outside, the night air felt **cool, refreshing, alive.**

I started walking, my mind surprisingly **silent.**

No anxious thoughts, no spiraling self-doubt—just **the quiet understanding that today had changed something in me.**

Maybe I didn't need to **have it all figured out.** Maybe I didn't need to **impress my boss every day.** Maybe confidence wasn't about **eliminating fear,** but about learning to **move forward despite it.**

I smiled.

For the first time in a long time, **I wasn't overthinking.**

I was just **living.**

And that, I realized, **was enough.**

Key Takeaways for Calming Overthinking

- **Most fears exist only in your mind.** In reality, things often turn out better than you expect.

- **Confidence doesn't come before action—it comes after.** You don't have to feel ready to take the first step.

- **Your boss is just another human.** The way you perceive authority changes when you stop overthinking and start seeing people for who they are.

- **Success isn't about never failing.** It's about moving forward, no matter how many times you mess up.

- **Cherish small wins.** They make the big ones possible.

- **Sometimes, the best way to calm your thoughts is to just be present—with work, with friends, with life.**

🚀 **Next Up → Finding Meaning in Your Thoughts**

Chapter 9

Finding Meaning in Your Thoughts

"Some of the best answers in life
don't come from thinking alone.
They come from conversations with people
who remind you who you are."

The Plan That Almost Didn't Happen

The thing about Aisha's plans? **They're never really plans.**

They start as half-serious suggestions, turn into aggressively pushed invitations, and somehow, **by the end of it, you find yourself in a completely different part of the city, wondering how you got there.**

This time, it was **Prinsep Ghat.**

10 PM. On a Tuesday.

"Are we really doing this?" I asked, phone pressed to my ear.

"Obviously," Aisha said, like I had just questioned gravity. "You need a **deep conversation under the stars. And I need mishti.**"

I sighed. "And Tanya?"

"She's already on board. And Aarav too. Don't be late."

And that was that.

One moment, I was wrapping up work, **mentally exhausted from another day of overthinking.** The next, I was sitting on a cold stone bench near the river, watching the Howrah Bridge glow in the distance, my friends beside me.

**"Some nights feel like stories waiting to be told.
This was one of them."**

Late-Night Conversations & Existential Debates

The wind was **cool against my face.** Kolkata looked different at night—**quieter, softer, more thoughtful.**

Tanya sat cross-legged on the bench, dipping a piece of **rosogolla into chai** like a criminal. Aarav leaned against the railing, scrolling through his phone, while Aisha, as expected, was **holding court.**

She was midway through **one of her theories about life.**

"...so basically," she was saying, waving a spoon dramatically, "all our problems would be solved if we just accepted that **life is random, people are weird, and nothing actually matters in the grand scheme of things.**"

Tanya rolled her eyes. "So your answer to everything is just **'stop caring'**?"

"Not stop caring," Aisha said. "**Stop overthinking.**"

My ears perked up.

Aarav glanced up from his phone. "That's rich coming from the person who once spent **two hours debating what caption to put on her Instagram post.**"

Aisha gasped. "That was a **serious** decision."

"Sure," Tanya smirked. "Because the world was waiting for your deep thoughts on biryani vs. pizza."

Aisha threw a sugar packet at her.

I smiled, shaking my head.

This was **our group.** This was **what made everything feel lighter.**

And yet, somewhere in the middle of all this nonsense, Aisha had a point.

"Overthinking makes small things feel big. Conversations make big things feel small."

Why Do We Overthink?

At some point, the jokes faded, and we fell into **a more serious kind of silence.**

The river stretched ahead, the lights of the city shimmering on its surface.

Tanya spoke first.

"Do you guys ever feel like… we're just existing on autopilot?" she asked, hugging her knees.

Aisha snorted. "Damn, Tanya. **That's a Tuesday night thought?"**

"I'm serious," she said. "Like… every day just feels like the same cycle. Work, sleep, think too much, repeat."

I stared at the river.

Yeah. **I knew that feeling too well.**

Aarav finally spoke. "That's because most of us are stuck in **thought loops.** We wake up, we replay the same doubts, the same 'what-ifs,' the same fears. And we don't even realize we're doing it."

Aisha exhaled. "Wow. So we're just… repeating old anxieties like a bad playlist?"

"Pretty much," Aarav said. "And the worst part? **We assume thinking about something over and over means we're solving it. But most of the time, we're just making ourselves miserable."**

I looked at him. "So what's the fix?"

Aarav shrugged. "Honestly? **Doing something different. Breaking the cycle.** Even something small. New routine, new hobby, new conversation."

Tanya nodded. "That's why nights like this help. They remind me that not everything is just... deadlines and existential dread."

Aisha dramatically put a hand on her chest. "Wow. **Is this growth? Are we becoming wise?**"

We laughed.

But deep down, **I knew we were onto something.**

**"Sometimes, you don't need an answer.
You just need a different perspective."**

Aisha's Unhinged Theory on Happiness

As usual, **Aisha decided we were getting too serious.**

"Alright," she said, clapping her hands. "Here's my latest theory: Happiness is just **expectation minus reality.**"

Aarav raised an eyebrow. "Elaborate."

"Think about it," she said. "If you expect a **10/10 day** but reality gives you a **6/10 day,** you feel miserable. But if you expected a **2/10 day** and got a **6/10 day,** you'd be thrilled. It's the same day, but your happiness depends on **what you expected.**"

Tanya stared at her. "Okay, that's actually... weirdly smart."

"Thank you," Aisha said. "I have **brief moments of genius.**"

I leaned back.

So maybe **happiness wasn't about controlling everything.**

Maybe it was just about **adjusting your expectations.**

"Sometimes, happiness is just about noticing the good instead of expecting the perfect."

The Realization That Stuck With Me

We sat there for another hour, talking about **everything and nothing.**

The night was **alive with possibilities**, but for once, I wasn't overthinking them.

I just let the conversation **be what it was.**

And in doing that, I felt something shift.

Maybe I had spent too long **waiting for certainty.**

For the perfect career plan, the perfect timing, the perfect version of myself that didn't doubt anything.

But maybe that version of me **didn't exist.**

Maybe life wasn't about **having it all figured out.**

Maybe it was just about **showing up, having conversations, and letting things unfold.**

Maybe that was enough.

"You don't need all the answers. You just need good friends, good conversations, and the courage to keep moving forward."

The Walk Back & What Stayed With Me

It was nearly **midnight** when we finally decided to leave.

The streets were quiet, the city **breathing softly under streetlights.**

Aisha was still debating **if biryani was an emotion,** Tanya was humming an old song, and Aarav was texting someone—probably Aisha.

As I walked, I realized something.

Not once tonight had I spiraled into overthinking.

Not once had I felt **stuck in my own head.**

Because **sometimes, the best cure for overthinking isn't deep analysis.**

It's **friendship, late-night walks, and the simple magic of being present.**

I smiled to myself.

Maybe I didn't need to know where life was going.

Maybe I just needed to **keep walking.**

Key Takeaways from the Night at Prinsep Ghat

- **You can't think your way out of overthinking.** Sometimes, you just need a change of scenery, a conversation, or a late-night walk.

- **Happiness is expectation minus reality.** Maybe we need to stop expecting life to be perfect and start noticing the small joys.

- **Thought loops keep you stuck.** If you keep replaying the same fears, change something—your routine, your mindset, your company.

- **Some of life's best answers come from conversations.** Not over-analysis, not overplanning—just talking to the right people at the right time.

- **The future will always be uncertain.** But maybe, just maybe, **you don't need to have it all figured out to be okay.**

And most importantly:

- **You are not alone.** No matter how lost you feel, there are always people, places, and conversations that will bring you back to yourself

🚀 **Next Up → Trusting Yourself in an Uncertain World**

Chapter 10

Trusting Yourself in an Uncertain World

**"You don't need to have all
the answers to move forward. Sometimes,
you just need to trust that you'll figure it
out along the way."**

The Quiet Night & A Restless Mind

The city had slowed down.

The usual chaos—the honking, the rush, the endless noise—had faded into a soft, distant hum. It was one of those nights when even Kolkata seemed to breathe slower.

I sat by my window, a warm cup of tea in my hands, watching the streetlights flicker.

It should have been peaceful.

But inside my head, **the storm hadn't stopped.**

I thought about work. **Even after a good day, why did I still feel like I wasn't doing enough?**

I thought about friendships. **How time was changing things—some people were growing closer, others drifting away.**

I thought about the past. **The mistakes, the things I should've said but didn't, the things I wish I could take back.**

And, as usual, my mind asked:

"Where is all of this going? Am I making the right choices? What happens next?"

The Call That Came at the Right Time

My phone buzzed.

I glanced at the screen. **Aisha.**

I almost didn't pick up.

Not because I didn't want to talk, but because **I wasn't in the mood for one of her chaotic monologues about life, the universe, or why biryani was an emotion.**

But something told me to answer.

"Hello?"

"You sound weird," she said immediately.

I sighed. "It's midnight. Of course, I sound weird."

"Uh-huh," she said, unimpressed. "Or maybe you're in one of your *deep overthinking modes* again?"

I didn't reply. Which, honestly, was enough of an answer.

The Problem with Always Searching for Certainty

Aisha sighed. "Okay, tell me. What's the existential crisis tonight?"

I hesitated. Then, instead of dodging the question, I told the truth.

"I don't know," I admitted. "I just feel like… I'm stuck. Like no matter how much I do, I'm always unsure if I'm doing enough. Or if I'm even on the right path."

There was a pause. Then:

"You know what your problem is?"

I rolled my eyes. "Here we go."

"You act like you're supposed to have **a perfect plan for everything.** Like there's a *right* way to do life and you're terrified of messing it up."

I exhaled. "Well... yeah?"

She groaned. "Okay, listen. Do you remember when we were kids, and we used to play in the rain?"

I frowned. "What?"

"Just answer."

I thought back. Long ago, when life was simpler, before responsibilities and worries took over.

"Yeah, I remember," I said. "Why?"

"Back then, did you stand in the rain, freaking out about whether you'd get wet? Or did you just... enjoy it?"

I blinked.

Aisha continued. "That's my point. Life is the same way. You don't stand there overthinking if the rain is good or bad, if you should take a calculated risk before stepping into it. You just **step out, get wet, and figure it out from there.**"

I was quiet.

Because damn.

The Moment It Clicked

Aisha sighed. "The thing is, you'll never have all the answers. No one does. Even the people who *look* like they have it all figured out? They don't."

I ran a hand through my hair. "So what do I do?"

"You **trust yourself** a little more."

"Easier said than done."

"I know," she said. "But think about it. Half the things you overthink? **They either won't matter in a few months, or they'll work out in ways you never expected.**"

I thought about that. About all the **nights I had spent stressing over things that never even happened.**

"You can't micromanage life," she added. "You just have to trust that whatever happens, you'll handle it. Just like you always have."

I let that sink in.

Maybe she was right. **Maybe trusting myself wasn't about being certain—it was about moving forward anyway.**

The Goodbye That Didn't Feel Like Goodbye

Aisha was still talking—something about how *biryani is proof that the universe wants us to be happy.*

I interrupted.

"Aisha?"

"Yeah?"

"Thank you."

She paused. "For what?"

"For making things make sense when they don't."

There was a beat of silence. Then she laughed.

"Oh my God. **Are you having an emotional moment?**" she teased. "Hold on, let me document this. I need proof for when you deny it later."

I groaned. "Good night, Aisha."

"Good night, Overthinker."

I hung up, shaking my head.

But smiling.

Because for the first time in a long time, **I wasn't searching for certainty.**

I wasn't waiting for a perfect plan to feel okay.

I was just **here.**

And tonight, **that was enough.**

Key Takeaways from This Night

- **Trust isn't about having all the answers. It's about knowing you'll figure it out along the way.**

- **Most of your worries won't even matter in six months. Don't waste your peace on them now.**

- **Some fears are just thoughts. Not reality. Not truth. Just passing doubts you don't have to listen to.**

- **A good friend can change everything. Keep the ones who remind you of who you are, not just who you're afraid to be.**

- **You don't need certainty to move forward. You just need to take the next step.**

The Final Goodbye to the Reader

Wherever you are, whatever is on your mind right now, just know this:

It's okay.

You don't need to fix everything tonight.

You don't need to figure out your whole life in one sitting.

You are allowed to be unsure. You are allowed to feel lost. But you are **also allowed to be happy—even in the middle of the unknown.**

So take a deep breath.

Let go of the things you don't need to carry anymore.

And trust yourself to figure out the rest.

You always do.

The End. But Also, The Beginning.

This is not the end of your story. It's just a reminder that **you get to write it however you want.**

The thoughts will come. The doubts will whisper.

But now?

Now, you know how to **let them go.**

Good night.

And more importantly—**good life.**

Final Note: If This Book Helped You...

If this book made you smile, think, or feel a little lighter, share it with someone who **overthinks at 2 AM just like you.**

Because the best thing about peace? **It grows when you pass it on.**

Your Truly

Satya Sankar Sahoo (P.S This is my first book)

About the Author – Satya Sankar Sahoo

Satya Sankar Sahoo is an entrepreneur, writer, thinker, and **self-proclaimed overthinker-turned-storyteller** who knows exactly what it's like to lie awake at 2AM, battling an endless loop of "what-ifs."

he found himself constantly **caught between ambition, self-doubt, and the chaos of modern life.** This book isn't just about overcoming overthinking—it's a collection of **real conversations, lived experiences, and the lessons learned along the way.**

Through humor, storytelling, and late-night realizations, **Satya hopes to remind readers that overthinking is just a part of the journey—but it doesn't have to define the destination.**

When he's not writing, you can probably find him **wandering through the streets of Kolkata, debating food choices with friends, or pretending to have life figured out.**

Connect with Satya on https://www.linkedin.com/in/satyasankarsahoo/

Before You Go... A Little Challenge From Me to You

You've made it to the end of *Calming 2AM Thoughts*—and I hope you now feel a little more understood, a little less alone, and a lot more ready to face those midnight spirals.

But here's the truth:

Reading is the first step. Real change comes from doing.

So I created something special for you.

☉ The 2AM Survival Toolkit + 15-Day Challenge

It's simple. For the next 15 days, I want you to:

- Spend 5-10 minutes each night with this toolkit

- Use the journal prompts, calming techniques, and mindset flips

- Try one small action to gently reclaim your peace

Whether it's writing down your 2AM thoughts, using the 90-second rule, or grounding yourself in the present—this challenge is your space to *practice* everything you've just read.

I'd love to hear from you.

✍ Let's Begin

Turn the page to find your 15-Day Challenge + 2AM Survival Toolkit.

This is your space. Your healing. Your story in the making.

I'll be cheering for you—quietly, from wherever I am—each night you choose peace over panic.

DATE: ________________   TIME: _______________

1. What thoughts are keeping me awake right now?

    → ____

    ____

2. Are they facts or feelings? (Circle one)

    → FACT / FEELING

3. Which method can I use tonight? (Check one)

    ☐ 90-Second Rule

    ☐ 5-4-3-2-1 Grounding

    ☐ "What's the worst that could happen?" game

    ☐ Write & Release method

4. Rewrite one negative thought into a better version:

    → From: "I'm not doing enough"

    → To: "I'm growing at my own pace"

5. How do I want to feel when I wake up tomorrow?

    → ____

    ____

☑ Small win from today: _______________________________

DATE: _______________   TIME: _______________

1. What thoughts are keeping me awake right now?

    → ____

    ____

2. Are they facts or feelings? (Circle one)

    → FACT / FEELING

3. Which method can I use tonight? (Check one)

    ☐ 90-Second Rule

    ☐ 5-4-3-2-1 Grounding

    ☐ "What's the worst that could happen?" game

    ☐ Write & Release method

4. Rewrite one negative thought into a better version:

    → From: "I'm not doing enough"

    → To: "I'm growing at my own pace"

5. How do I want to feel when I wake up tomorrow?

    → ____

    ____

☑ Small win from today: _______________________________

DATE: _______________   TIME: _______________

1. What thoughts are keeping me awake right now?

    → ____

    ____

2. Are they facts or feelings? (Circle one)

    → FACT / FEELING

3. Which method can I use tonight? (Check one)

    ☐ 90-Second Rule

    ☐ 5-4-3-2-1 Grounding

    ☐ "What's the worst that could happen?" game

    ☐ Write & Release method

4. Rewrite one negative thought into a better version:

    → From: "I'm not doing enough"

    → To: "I'm growing at my own pace"

5. How do I want to feel when I wake up tomorrow?

    → ____

    ____

☑ Small win from today: _______________________________

DATE: ______________   TIME: ______________

1. What thoughts are keeping me awake right now?

    → ____

    ____

2. Are they facts or feelings? (Circle one)

    → FACT / FEELING

3. Which method can I use tonight? (Check one)

    ☐ 90-Second Rule

    ☐ 5-4-3-2-1 Grounding

    ☐ "What's the worst that could happen?" game

    ☐ Write & Release method

4. Rewrite one negative thought into a better version:

    → From: "I'm not doing enough"

    → To: "I'm growing at my own pace"

5. How do I want to feel when I wake up tomorrow?

    → ____

    ____

☑ Small win from today: ____________________________

DATE: _______________   TIME: _______________

1. What thoughts are keeping me awake right now?

    → ____

    ____

2. Are they facts or feelings? (Circle one)

    → FACT / FEELING

3. Which method can I use tonight? (Check one)

    ☐ 90-Second Rule

    ☐ 5-4-3-2-1 Grounding

    ☐ "What's the worst that could happen?" game

    ☐ Write & Release method

4. Rewrite one negative thought into a better version:

    → From: "I'm not doing enough"

    → To: "I'm growing at my own pace"

5. How do I want to feel when I wake up tomorrow?

    → ____

    ____

☑ Small win from today: _______________________________

DATE: ________________   TIME: ________________

1. What thoughts are keeping me awake right now?

    → ____

    ____

2. Are they facts or feelings? (Circle one)

    → FACT / FEELING

3. Which method can I use tonight? (Check one)

    ☐ 90-Second Rule

    ☐ 5-4-3-2-1 Grounding

    ☐ "What's the worst that could happen?" game

    ☐ Write & Release method

4. Rewrite one negative thought into a better version:

    → From: "I'm not doing enough"

    → To: "I'm growing at my own pace"

5. How do I want to feel when I wake up tomorrow?

    → ____

    ____

☑ Small win from today: ______________________________

DATE: _______________   TIME: _______________

1. What thoughts are keeping me awake right now?

    → ____

    ____

2. Are they facts or feelings? (Circle one)

    → FACT / FEELING

3. Which method can I use tonight? (Check one)

    ☐ 90-Second Rule

    ☐ 5-4-3-2-1 Grounding

    ☐ "What's the worst that could happen?" game

    ☐ Write & Release method

4. Rewrite one negative thought into a better version:

    → From: "I'm not doing enough"

    → To: "I'm growing at my own pace"

5. How do I want to feel when I wake up tomorrow?

    → ____

    ____

☑ Small win from today: _______________________

DATE: ______________   TIME: ______________

1. What thoughts are keeping me awake right now?

    → ____

    ____

2. Are they facts or feelings? (Circle one)

    → FACT / FEELING

3. Which method can I use tonight? (Check one)

    ☐ 90-Second Rule

    ☐ 5-4-3-2-1 Grounding

    ☐ "What's the worst that could happen?" game

    ☐ Write & Release method

4. Rewrite one negative thought into a better version:

    → From: "I'm not doing enough"

    → To: "I'm growing at my own pace"

5. How do I want to feel when I wake up tomorrow?

    → ____

    ____

☑ Small win from today: ___________________________

DATE: _____________   TIME: _____________

1. What thoughts are keeping me awake right now?

    → ____

    ____

2. Are they facts or feelings? (Circle one)

    → FACT / FEELING

3. Which method can I use tonight? (Check one)

    ☐ 90-Second Rule

    ☐ 5-4-3-2-1 Grounding

    ☐ "What's the worst that could happen?" game

    ☐ Write & Release method

4. Rewrite one negative thought into a better version:

    → From: "I'm not doing enough"

    → To: "I'm growing at my own pace"

5. How do I want to feel when I wake up tomorrow?

    → ____

    ____

☑ Small win from today: _______________________________

DATE: ________________   TIME: ________________

1. What thoughts are keeping me awake right now?

    → ____

    ____

2. Are they facts or feelings? (Circle one)

    → FACT / FEELING

3. Which method can I use tonight? (Check one)

    ☐ 90-Second Rule

    ☐ 5-4-3-2-1 Grounding

    ☐ "What's the worst that could happen?" game

    ☐ Write & Release method

4. Rewrite one negative thought into a better version:

    → From: "I'm not doing enough"

    → To: "I'm growing at my own pace"

5. How do I want to feel when I wake up tomorrow?

    → ____

    ____

☑ Small win from today: ________________________________

DATE: _______________   TIME: _______________

1. What thoughts are keeping me awake right now?

    → ____

    ____

2. Are they facts or feelings? (Circle one)

    → FACT / FEELING

3. Which method can I use tonight? (Check one)

    ☐ 90-Second Rule

    ☐ 5-4-3-2-1 Grounding

    ☐ "What's the worst that could happen?" game

    ☐ Write & Release method

4. Rewrite one negative thought into a better version:

    → From: "I'm not doing enough"

    → To: "I'm growing at my own pace"

5. How do I want to feel when I wake up tomorrow?

    → ____

    ____

☑ Small win from today: _______________________

DATE: ______________   TIME: ______________

1. What thoughts are keeping me awake right now?

    → ____

    ____

2. Are they facts or feelings? (Circle one)

    → FACT / FEELING

3. Which method can I use tonight? (Check one)

    ☐ 90-Second Rule

    ☐ 5-4-3-2-1 Grounding

    ☐ "What's the worst that could happen?" game

    ☐ Write & Release method

4. Rewrite one negative thought into a better version:

    → From: "I'm not doing enough"

    → To: "I'm growing at my own pace"

5. How do I want to feel when I wake up tomorrow?

    → ____

    ____

☑ Small win from today: ______________________________

DATE: _______________   TIME: _______________

1. What thoughts are keeping me awake right now?

    → ____

    ____

2. Are they facts or feelings? (Circle one)

    → FACT / FEELING

3. Which method can I use tonight? (Check one)

    ☐ 90-Second Rule

    ☐ 5-4-3-2-1 Grounding

    ☐ "What's the worst that could happen?" game

    ☐ Write & Release method

4. Rewrite one negative thought into a better version:

    → From: "I'm not doing enough"

    → To: "I'm growing at my own pace"

5. How do I want to feel when I wake up tomorrow?

    → ____

    ____

☑ Small win from today: _______________________________

DATE: _______________   TIME: _______________

1. What thoughts are keeping me awake right now?

    → ____

    ____

2. Are they facts or feelings? (Circle one)

    → FACT / FEELING

3. Which method can I use tonight? (Check one)

    ☐ 90-Second Rule

    ☐ 5-4-3-2-1 Grounding

    ☐ "What's the worst that could happen?" game

    ☐ Write & Release method

4. Rewrite one negative thought into a better version:

    → From: "I'm not doing enough"

    → To: "I'm growing at my own pace"

5. How do I want to feel when I wake up tomorrow?

    → ____

    ____

☑ Small win from today: _______________________________

DATE: _______________   TIME: _______________

1. What thoughts are keeping me awake right now?

    → ____

    ____

2. Are they facts or feelings? (Circle one)

    → FACT / FEELING

3. Which method can I use tonight? (Check one)

    ☐ 90-Second Rule

    ☐ 5-4-3-2-1 Grounding

    ☐ "What's the worst that could happen?" game

    ☐ Write & Release method

4. Rewrite one negative thought into a better version:

    → From: "I'm not doing enough"

    → To: "I'm growing at my own pace"

5. How do I want to feel when I wake up tomorrow?

    → ____

    ____

☑ Small win from today: _______________________________

🌐 Want More? Let's Stay Connected.

This isn't the end — it's just the beginning of our late-night journey.

👉 Scan the QR code or visit calming2amthoughts.in **to:**

- Join the **2AM Thoughts Community**

- Download **free bonus toolkits** and calming resources

- Share your reflections or find others who *get it*

- Be part of a space where overthinkers feel safe, heard, and human

This book may end here. But your story of letting go is just getting started.

I'll see you on the other side.

With warmth,

Satya Sankar Sahoo